YOUR FIRST DEAL A TO Z

#1 Real Estate Wholesaling Book from Start to Finish

> How to make $10,000 in the next
> 21 days with no money

BY

JOSEPH COELLO

ABOUT THE AUTHOR

This is the part of the book where I answer some important questions before you spend the next hour or two reading what I've written.

1. Why should you read this book?
2. What makes this book different than any other wholesale guide or content available online?
3. Why am I qualified to teach you how to wholesale?

Well firstly, you should read this book if you have an interest in wholesaling, or assignable contracts.

Or, if you have little starting money and want to get some serious cash, and experience so you can invest yourself in real estate.

This book sets itself apart from other guides or content easily available online because we intend for you to be able to read this, and realistically close a deal with no further input from us. Of course, we'd love for you to become a student of ours and really work with you one on one to make you great. But the general purpose of this book is to get you a deal under your belt, taking you from A to Z through the entire process. You'll be able to do this using free or cheap methods, meaning you can start with nothing and create a real income stream for yourself to support your family.

If you're still reading, you still have an interest in learning the methods on how to start wholesaling for yourself. Why should I be your teacher?

My bio: I was born in Queens, NY the oldest of 4 boys to two hardworking parents. When I was in elementary school we moved down to Central Florida where I learned how to surf and lived a suburban lifestyle. When I was 17, I graduated high school and joined the Army. I did 6 years in the service, mainly as a medic in the elite 1st Ranger Battalion, where I deployed to Afghanistan two times. During this time, I also was lucky enough to have two beautiful children. When my time in the service ended, I moved to Florida to be closer to my children, and bought my first property using my VA mortgage. The pursuit of higher education in the form of Physician Assistant school pulled me to Buffalo, NY. I got two masters degrees while up there but as soon as I moved, I made an important market realization that everyone else already knew.

It was there where I started noticing a real estate market much more dynamic than the pulse of the market in Brevard county, FL. Partnering with my brother, we got a 5-unit rental property. From there I realized that there was much more money to be made in real estate than in medicine, and I enjoyed it more. I got my real estate license to begin networking with the right people and to learn more formal skills about real estate in the area. I began working with clients with total independence and little oversight under a small brokerage. It was daunting, I had no roadmap and no one holding my hand. I was able to excel under these conditions with hard work and extreme self-awareness. I started closing a lot of deals and earned a solid reputation with some community leaders. Gaining knowledge of how deals worked, and how contracts were written after each failed or successful: showing, negotiation, inspection and closing.

The market up in Buffalo, NY was very tough. Investment properties with high cash flow were selling in under a week on the market. Some sold the same day they hit the market, with all cash offers, no inspection and over asking price. It was truly unique and unforgiving. In these ultra-competitive conditions, the average investor (me at the time), was unable to purchase anything! I didn't have $50,000 to $200,000 cash to buy rental properties with! I thought I was big shit because I was pre-approved for a 20% down mortgage, but quickly felt too broke to make moves upward.

I noticed many of my clients I worked with using my real estate license were also in the same boat. My idea at the time was simple. If these houses were selling so quick before they hit the market, the only way I could get my clients a property, and myself the listing – was to find the houses BEFORE they hit the market.

I now had another problem; I didn't want to just be finding all these deals and not get any part of these deals. After all, I started this journey to be a real estate Investor, not a real estate worker. The initial issue was I didn't have enough CASH to get into the best deals myself.

My main strategy to solve this problem was to partner with other investors or clients that had the same issue. We all wanted those $300,000 rental properties with 19% cap rates, but we couldn't compete with all cash offers. Together we had enough cash for these deals. My investors were hesitant though, after all I was new to real estate, why should they trust in my skills to assess a good deal, to manage the property, and structure the deal. I had to prove myself before anyone would give me an ounce of trust with their money, and rightfully so.

I started my own real estate business at this point in the story, finding potential sellers of these off-market deals. I began focusing on marketing techniques, trying every method known to the first 50 pages of google and any other creative way I could think of to find sellers and off market deals. Nothing was ever better than word of mouth referrals, but its still very necessary to actively market.

After employing these methods to market, we'd keep the best fix and flips for wholesaling (a technique I learned about as an agent). Making between $5,000 to $25,000 per assignment or wholesale deal at the time. (That's what I'll teach you how to do). Investing all of the profit from each deal into the business I was able to scale and grow, hiring more employees and closing more deals.

Anything that was suitable for a buy and hold was kept aside for my real estate company to close on. Allowing our partners and investors to join in on the best off-market deals that we would find. Giving monthly distributions of the rent to our partners and investors on these deals at

16%+ cap rates keeps them all very happy and always asking about the next deal.

Today I am kept busy running the real estate investment company, primarily scouting for the next deal to bring to the partners invited to invest with me, while business partners and employees maintain wholesale operations, renovations and management of long term and short-term rentals.

After several years in the industry, and having closed countless deals. I decided it is time to fully pass down all knowledge I have about how to successfully find and close a wholesale deal from start to finish. And above all, how to do it with style, class and finesse.

If you want to learn how to wholesale, and want to be leaps and bounds above the majority of the time-wasters out there wholesaling, then this is the book for you.

TABLE OF CONTENTS

About the Author i

Steps to Wholesaling & Wholetailing i

    Wholesaling Explained iii

Become Self-Aware 6

Create a large buyers list 8

    Ways to get hot buyer leads 12

        Bandit Signs 13

        For Sale Signs 15

        Craigslist ads 17

        Popular real estate listing websites 21

        Social Media 24

            LinkedIn 24

            Facebook 26

    Confidence 27

Working with Attorneys and Title Companies 29

Search for Sellers 35

Ways to find sellers 36

Craigslist ads 37

    Craigslist – For Sale 38

    Craigslist - For Rent 39

    Craigslist – Posting Ads 40

Public records websites 41

    Absentee owners 43

    LLC owners 43

    Same owner multiple houses 43

    Probates 44

Mailing Campaigns 44

Driving streets 48

FSBO websites 49

Auctions 56

Social Media 57

    Facebook 57

    LinkedIn 58

Real Estate Investor Meetups 60

Violations list 60

Industry professionals 61

    Attorneys 62

    Section 8 housing lists 63

    Title Companies 63

    Property managers 64

    Real estate agents & Wholesalers 65

Make educated offers – Intro to a CMA 68

Comparative Market Analysis (CMA) 70

    Search Filters 71

    ARV 72

    Pulling Comps 73

Quickly Estimating Repairs 76

    What is a Good Deal? 81

Getting your offer Accepted 84

    What should I say? 85

Contingencies and other types of Contracts 87

Hard to Close Sellers 89

Why should they work with you?..
92

Authority...
97

Send the property to your buyers 99

Collect your deposit check / assignment fee ....
101

After you Assign the Contract 105

Managing the Deal ....
106

Finding the next one 109

Being your Own Boss ....
110

Finding a Mentor ....
110

STEPS TO WHOLESALING & WHOLETAILING

My name is Joe Coello, and I love real estate. And if I accomplish the mission of this book, soon you, the reader, will too.

One of the most frequent questions that I get asked, is "How can I invest in real estate if I don't have enough money to buy a house?" That is a great question, and the options are there if you are willing to be creative.

That's what everyone says at least, when you look at unconventional methods of controlling real property. You really don't need to get creative; we aren't re-inventing anything here - the methods are in place if you know how to structure the deal.

I'm 100% serious. If you implement the tools and skills in this book, you can be collecting $5,000-$10,000 cash in the next 14 days – or more once the house actually closes.

Wholesaling and Wholetailing are great methods to get involved in real estate if you have little to no cash. You have the choice to wholesale in your local market or you can use the power of the internet and virtual wholesale anywhere in America. To sum up what these words mean:

Wholesaling is when you submit an offer on a property and get it under contract. This contract is specially prepared to be legally assignable, so you can sell this contract - or promise to buy the house - to an end buyer (or assignee). You collect the difference.

Wholetailing is when you make improvements to the property, and then either list the property on the MLS, or sell it to a buyer that you find using the methods that I will show you later on.

[If a home is listed on the multiple listing service (MLS) that means a real estate agent has an "Agency" agreement signed with that owner. This is an agreement that a real estate agent and property owner sign that gives the real estate agent control over selling the house, and ensures they make their commission no matter who buys the home.]

Wholesaling is a great method to make tons of profit and gain a wealth of experience in real estate, not to mention learn everything about your local market.

But remember, if it were easy, everyone would do it - and you'll see everyone and their uncle tries to wholesale because the barriers to entry are so low.

You will have a ton of competition, but so few people do it well, so your chance to become a market leader is absolutely a reality. Whether you chose to wholesale the traditional way or if you want to become a virtual wholesaler, the only limit is your own work ethic, and your sales ability.

WHOLESALING EXPLAINED

To quickly sum up what wholesaling is:

You are finding a house that is off the market meaning is not represented or listed a by real estate agent.

You build rapport with the seller/owner of the house and do a quick inspection of the property.

You determine the value of the home, estimate the repairs needed to bring it to the full market value, and make an offer on the property that you know will leave you some profit (leave room for a reasonable mark-up).

The offer is written on an assignable contract, meaning you can assign the terms of the contract to whoever you would like. Then the offer gets accepted.

You then "assign" the contract to a buyer that you find. You do this with a one-page agreement that you and the "end-buyer" sign.

The buyer that you found is paying for the home at a more expensive price than what you are paying for.

That buyer now is the person who has the contract to buy the house.

You collect the difference in price as your fee.

Meaning you have an off-market property and the seller wants $65,000. You negotiate and they accept $50,000. You list the property for sale and market to your buyers at

$60,000. When your buyer accepts your price at 60k, you collect the 10k difference – either up front as a deposit, or at closing as the assignment fee.

Everyone makes money, everyone is happy.

I just made this process seem very easy, but in reality, it will require you to combine all of your people skills, all of your salesmanship skills, and is a culmination of all of the positive traits that you have acquired as you've gone through life.

It is not an entry level skill. You need to know how to find a property, convince the owner to sell, value the property and price the repairs. On top of that you need to quickly find a serious and qualified end-buyer to buy the deal from you.

You need to do all of this within a few days to weeks at the most. If you follow my guide, you'll find yourself with a stack of cash in your hands in the next 2 weeks.

It is my goal that after you are done reading this, you will be able to find your own deals and pay off all your monthly bills with a few days' worth of hard work – so you can be your own boss and work for yourself full time.

If you have any issues along the way, my team of expert consultants are always available to mentor you through any deal you may have and ensure a smooth and profitable closing.

We can guide you through the door of success, but you need to take the first step. If you are willing to invest your valuable time, you can receive returns in the form of experience and most importantly – *MONEY* – from real estate.

BECOME SELF-AWARE

I'm not going to tell you how important a first impression is. Do you know how you are coming off to other people? Most importantly in this instance: How are you being perceived by your clients? The property owners and the property buyers need to take you serious and understand that you know what you are talking about.

What types of people do you take serious? Professionals. How do professionals like lawyers and doctors talk to you? They state the facts and why the facts are the way they are. They have polished appearances. The way they speak reflects their education level and general confidence.

You don't need a college degree, but understand that the people you are working with in this industry are often times very sharp individuals, you don't get to be rich and own a lot of property by being a dummy (most times).

The facts of the matter is: people won't let you get their house under contract if you aren't being perceived as an expert and a professional. You do this by building rapport, and by SOUNDING good. Remember – the first time most people interact with you, is on the phone.

Having authority in your voice, not stuttering and trembling when you speak is just the bare minimum requirements to sounding good when making outbound and receiving inbound calls. If you are anxious about human interaction on the phone or in person then the only way to overcome this is by practicing these interactions out loud in your own time. Start off talking to a wall or a mirror, then promote yourself to a friend or family member once you have your script down pat.

Learn how to read your audience, and when to talk with slang and when not to. When to wear a suit, and when jeans and sneakers are appropriate. Know when to use the appropriate inflection in your voice and be aware if you appear friendly when you speak.

Have a variety of things to talk about with people in a wide range of subjects. Become personable, and keep a smile on your face. Also know when to freestyle and deviate from the script, stay loose and free, this shouldn't feel dreadful or hard to do – like a conversation with a friend.

Take baby steps to positively work on your outward projection towards the world and how you are perceived, and over time you will be a smooth talking and sharp looking real estate investor and wholesaler.

CREATE A LARGE BUYERS LIST

There are many methods to creating a list of buyers. Something that is very important to keep in mind is that this is a general list of real estate investors. Buyers are Sellers, and Sellers are Buyers. Build rapport with the people in your rolodex.

I listed this as the first step, but in reality, you need to be constantly building your buyers list, and your sellers list at the same time.

Your network in this industry is the only tool you need to leverage massive wealth.

You need to build and maintain rapport! What does this mean? It means that your reputation is everything. Talk to people like you normally do. If you are anti-social, the time for that, needs to end now. Your real estate business will suffer because of it.

How do you build rapport? Talk about their family, talk about what they do for a living, what hobbies do they have? What did they do last weekend? You get the idea. You will get a huge number of leads from word of mouth, so make sure you get things done right the first time and people will send their friends and family your way.

Very early in my career I negotiated some great deals for some very devout religious clients. I really busted my ass to make sure their deals closed quickly and to make sure the price point ensured a happy outcome for the buyer that I was representing.

Two weeks later my phone would not stop ringing from members of their religious congregation trying to get me to find them deals and work for them. I later found one of my best clients in that congregation and we are still closing deals together to this day.

Everyone that calls, texts or emails me about property goes into my "rolodex."

Do you have a rolodex yet?

If you don't you won't be successful in real estate. I started out with a google sheets document. I preferred using sheets at first, before switching to a CRM software that is dedicated to managing client relationships.

Using an excel style "google sheets" page to enter information of anyone who contacts you about real estate is a great method when first starting out. You can access the data anywhere because it is stored on google drive. You can also enter and retrieve info from your laptop or mobile phone.

I highly recommend using the template that I provide to make your own rolodex to start logging all the buyers and sellers that you talk to.

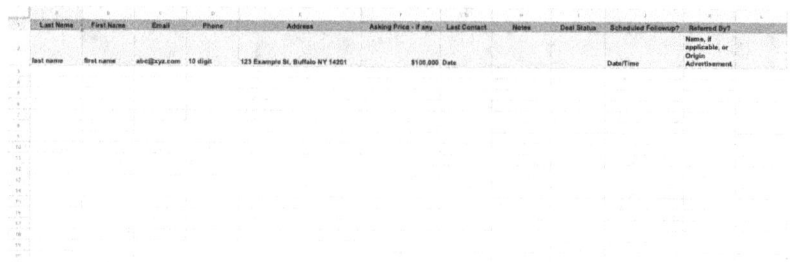

In reality, any method that works for you, and allows you to stay organized is all that you need.

The bigger your rolodex, the more deals will come your way, and the easier it will be for you to wholesale property.

You NEED to set aside a time every day, or every couple of days to sort through the numbers and text messages in your phone and transfer the data to your rolodex. We call this "synching the rolodex."

You will find that 99% of the time you will get an email, text message or phone call when you are not near your computer. When I am away from my laptop, or out driving and I get a call from a prospective client, what I will usually do is tell them: "Hey before we go, since I'm driving, would you mind sending me a text with your name and email address?"

Most times I get a text message a few seconds later with all the info I need to sync my rolodex once I get back to the office. If you don't sync your rolodex, you are going to lose contact info. If they never text you, be sure to remember to go back in your call log and save their number. I like to save their name, and property address under company info.

You'd be surprised how many people refuse to work with anyone who goes back on their word, even slightly. If you tell someone you're going to call them back, and forget to do it, you potentially just lost a client.

That means you just lost a business relationship that could have potentially netted you millions of dollars in profit over the span of working together. I've seen it happen over and over again. Don't lose business over preventable issues, all it takes is for you to take that extra step.

Be disciplined and set aside time for yourself to sync your rolodex, call back your buyers, and actively seek out sellers. Be consistent and you will find yourself among the top 1% of wholesalers in your area.

I have daily tasks written in sharpie on a dry erase board in the office. The team does these tasks as soon as they arrive:

- Check social media
- Check missed calls, voicemails and texts
- Send out mass texts
- Send out email blasts
- f/u on appointments
- cold calls
- renew leads
- update calendar
- update crm/rolodex

I suggest you get into a routine so your business can operate to its fullest capacity.

WAYS TO GET HOT BUYER LEADS.

Something that always pissed me off when I was broke was the fact that every "how to" guide was that they always seemed like scams to get your money.

I'll show you a few methods of lead generation that cost money. But for the most part, if you're just starting out, I know you'll prefer the free methods.

You can spend money to get buyers and sellers after you make some profit from the free leads that I show you how to generate.

Just trust in the process and stay confident, because very soon these buyers will be looking at the homes you will be sending them.

Treat each person responding to your marketing, like they're a millionaire. First of all, they really might be, and secondly, it's the right way to go about life. This is an essential step in becoming a wealthy real estate professional.

Each phone call you get from here on out is money calling you. People will be calling you, asking to pay you – by buying a house from you. Help them make it happen by giving them the types of property they are looking for.

BANDIT SIGNS

You see them all over, those little corrugated plastic signs that are staked into patches of grass by the road or stapled high up on wooden telephone poles.

Bandit signs work pretty well to generate leads and to help make sure you phone is always ringing. If you want to grow buyers list, bandit signs can be a great method to do this.

You can make signs to find seller leads too, but if you are in an area with a bunch of signs with similar formats like "Mike buys ugly houses", then I'd stick with another method for sellers.

Those signs are oftentimes made by another wholesaler, and like I say all the time – 99% of wholesalers out there are downright terrible at this job. Competition is a great thing. Rise above the crowd with signs that stand out. Your sign needs to appeal to your target audience.

I have used bandit signs before to get leads, and I did get a ton of calls. Bandit sign leads tend to give you a certain demographic of flippers that are generally looking for low price property.

No matter what, when you place a sign you are going to get a percentage of people who are just calling so that they can "kick the tires" so to speak. The main people that I get calling me from the bandit signs were investors and real estate agents.

Exactly the types of people who you want calling you.

Don't buy pre-made bandit signs, they are just overpriced and a waste of money. You only need a few signs when you are just starting out anyway. You can find them at Home Depot, Lowes and Walmart.

They should only cost $5 at the most per sign.

It is always good to have a few different signs with different variations of the same message. If you want to try between hand-written or stencil letters, that is also another variation you can make.

If you want to make bandit signs that actually get calls you need to follow this general template:

- Use brightly colored signs for your area
    - I use white and yellow signs. I use white in areas that are very green. But like I said, I live up north. When it snows, its best to use yellow or orange signs.
- Hand write your signs, don't buy the expensive ones that are pre-printed
    - This creates a fear of missing out when a buyer calls your sign. When someone sees a neatly printed sign that has a generic message about buying houses, they don't call it.
    - They barely recognize the sign; it just blends in with the background advertising static

that is the scenery at many busy intersections across American towns.

- If you don't have a house yet but still need to grow a buyers list: Sell what you want to have – don't be broad, be specific.
    - If you are targeting investors who want to buy for their own portfolio, make a bandit sign saying something along the lines of "3/3 duplex for sale $75,000 (555) 555-5555"
    - If you want to sell to a flipper or someone looking for a home to live in try "3/2/2 Single family near (nice area) $75,000"

Some jurisdictions have workers that scan the sides of the roads for these signs and remove them or may try and fine you. Please check in with your local laws so you don't get a bill in the mail or bring un-necessary stress to your life. Anecdotally, I knew a guy who would place his signs on a Friday evening after the city crews were off work. This allowed him all weekend before they removed them on Monday.

FOR SALE SIGNS

A really creative way that you can use to get leads is to actually place a for sale sign in your own front yard. It really works best if you own the property. But even if you rent, all you have to do is just ask your landlord if you can place a for rent sign in the yard so that you can start to collect leads for your real estate business.

With the "For Sale" sign in your front yard, or in your window, people will start calling you asking if your place is for sale.

Just follow our incoming call phone script and they'll be another buyer to add to your rolodex.

Many people in this industry are really quick to dish out the negativity, and they love to spread their hate with this method.

At the end of the day, you are new to this. You don't have the marketing budget that many other people do if they have several deals under their belt.

Do the best with what you've got. Don't let naysayers and negative people discourage you from implementing methods like this.

They may scoff at you; but at the end of the day, this method of lead generation can easily make you several thousand dollars. Re-invest that into a more sophisticated lead generation method once you close some deals.

Rolodex everyone that calls and use the scripts that we've given you and you will find a lot of success with this method.

CRAIGSLIST ADS

We use craigslist to find buyers and sellers. Initially, when you are building a list of buyers, you're going to use a method called posting "ghost ads"

This means that you are advertising a house that you don't have yet.

Take a trip to your ideal neighborhood to wholesale in. For my area, it is all over the city because the revitalization effort is still strongly underway.

Take a picture of a crappy house, but make sure there are no identifying features in the picture.

- Create a craigslist account

- Post a new ad in the "housing by owner section"

please limit each posting to a single area and category, once per 48 hours

what type of posting is this: (see prohibited list before posting.)

- ○ job offered
- ○ gig offered (I'm hiring for a short-term, small or odd job)
- ○ resume / job wanted

- ○ housing offered
- ○ housing wanted

- Pick "real estate - by owner"

please choose a category: (see prohibited list before posting.)

- ○ rooms & shares
- ○ apts/housing for rent (no shares, roommates, or sublets please!)
- ○ housing swap
- ○ office & commercial
- ○ parking & storage
- ○ real estate - by broker
- ○ real estate - by owner
- ○ sublets & temporary
- ○ vacation rentals

[continue]

- We are looking to create a large list of people looking to buy property quickly. So, we need to make titles that will draw that crowd in.

- Ads work better if your title references the local market

  ex:

- - "3/3 east side duplex for sale"
  - "Great Triplex near Bayside for sale"
  - "3/2 west side duplex for sale"
- Body:

  > 3/3 duplex for sale
  >
  > 3 bed 1 bath per side
  >
  > each side rented at $500 a side
  >
  > we have many other properties available
  >
  > OR
  >
  > 3/2/2 SFH near the College
  >
  > Perfect for rehabbers or flippers
  >
  > new roof, all new plumbing and electric
  >
  > ready for a fast closing!

- Put a Price that is low for the area but not too low
  - You want investors to call you. If you put the price too low, you're still going to get calls, but the conversation is going to start with "why is that price so low, what's wrong with the house?"
- Put an accurate zip code
- Fill in all the posting details

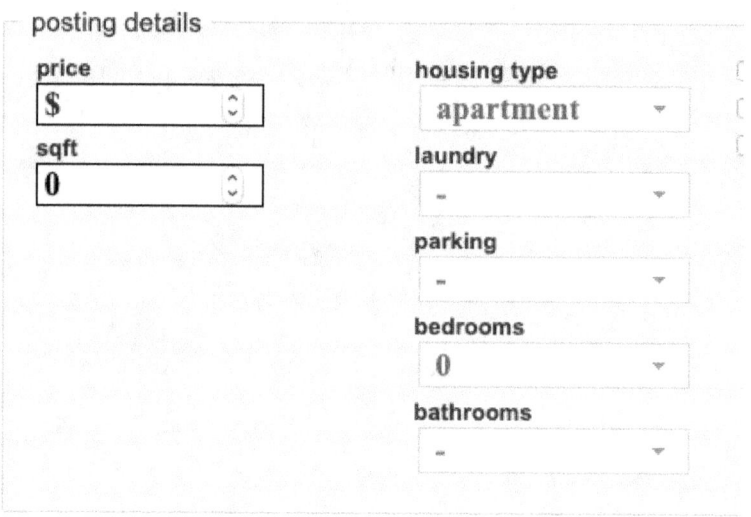

- List your name, number and email
- Post one (1) picture of a property
    - Don't post more than 2 pictures. You want people to call you so you can rolodex them. You do not want to answer all the questions they have with your ad. They need to feel like they have questions they must call you with.
- Be ready to put people into the rolodex when you post the ad
    - Have your google sheets page bookmarked so you can quickly pull it up when people call you.

POPULAR REAL ESTATE LISTING WEBSITES

One of the best methods I had in my toolbox to get leads, was something I noticed when I was first starting my career in real estate.

I realized when I got my first listing as a licensed real estate agent, and posted it on the MLS, the extreme potential there was as to reach people looking to spend money on property. As long as you were able to access the same network that all real estate agents can access, you could potentially have those same buyers calling you.

That's because the MLS automatically posts your listing onto all of these sites. I found that many of the people calling me had seen my listing on Zillow.

The internet really removed the need for anyone to get a real estate license. Companies like Zillow spend hundreds of thousands of dollars advertising and ensuring they are the top results in google searches.

How can you beat that?

Having access to list homes on Zillow and Trulia, really helped to expand my network. Websites like these and other for sale by owner websites, have high visibility to buyers and sellers alike.

For these sites, you shouldn't post ghost ads about properties you don't have some involvement with.

As a new wholesaler I realize that you may not have any property to list, but you can get away with posting your place, or your parents place a few times as a "FSBO" or "For Sale by Owner".

Just be sure to put your contact info in the description of the home for those sites. For an even better response, also take a picture of your "For Sale by Owner" sign with your phone number clearly written on it and upload that as the second picture.

If you don't, then no one will be able to contact you. Zillow basically hides your info.

- **For sale by owner** | **Zestimate®**: $135,997
Est. payment: $715/mo 💲 Get pre-qualified

> **Get more info**

The "get more info" buttons that Zillow puts near your FSBO listing will send your buyers to a real estate agent.

REMEMBER THIS FACT LATER ON

Zillow will route any interested buyers to the cell phones of real estate agents who pay them thousands for monthly advertising and "warm leads". So put your name and number and email in a visible spot in the description.

Try not to fill these sites with ghost ads, I really recommend only posting a home here that you live in or that you have under contract.

To post a home on Zillow, just type in the address. You should see two tabs in the top left part of the screen.

Click the owner view tab.

Click the button that says you own and manage the rental.

Then click the list home drop down menu and select one of the options. List for sale by owner is most likely your best bet to get your house up there. Just make sure you follow all the instructions above and make your contact info very easy to find.

SOCIAL MEDIA

We expand more on social media when we talk about finding sellers, but social media is also a great tool to use to find buyers.

LinkedIn and Facebook are among the best two sites to reach large numbers of people who are interested in investing in real estate.

You can sell a home very quickly if you utilize the power of Facebook marketplace and Facebook groups.

LinkedIn

LinkedIn allows you to search for people with "real estate" or "real estate investor" or any combination that you can think of that targets people who may want to buy from you – or sell to you.

Now is a great time to start adding people to your connections list on LinkedIn.

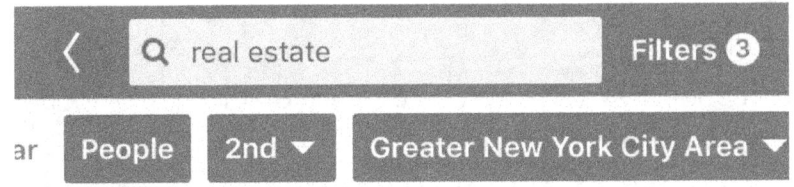

This is an example of the type of filters you should set when searching for investors. Instead of "real estate" you can add whatever niche of buyer you are looking for. Dentists, doctors, real estate investors – anyone with disposable income who is looking to buy some property from you.

Set the filter to people, so you are only searching for humans.

Set the other filter to 2nd degree connections, so you can instantly add them by pressing the plus sign, and also set the location to the area nearest to you.

Then, every day, add the max limit of people in that sub group that you are search through.

Now make ghost ad posts about the property you have for sale, and rolodex the people who contact you.

We use a special program for LinkedIn that automatically collects the contact information of our connections and rolodexes them for us, it really saves us a lot of time.

Students under our mentorship have access to these programs and any other paid resource we use on a daily basis to find and close deals.

Facebook

Facebook is a great resource – if not the best - to find buyers and sellers.

The method with Facebook, is to join groups that are specific to people buying and selling. Also join large local groups, and local groups that might have a theme, like sports or neighborhood activity.

Garage sale groups, barter groups, yard sale groups and other sales themed groups are perfect for what we want.

If you join too many groups too quickly, they will block you, so don't go crazy.

Once you are in a few groups, you can post messages about property you have for sale, and it'll get posted to all the groups you select.

Use the same template as the craigslist ad. This will guarantee that you get a response for your buyer's posts on Facebook.

Once you do get people to call you, you can use our script to get them in your rolodex.

Once you get more advanced you can start making a business page, and start posting buyer and seller marketing ads in groups.

Facebook has a robust marketing platform, I mean, its main revenue source is from people like me and you paying for advertisement. It links well with Instagram, so create a business Instagram while you're at it.

Design some tester social media ad campaigns, and run them with target demographics in place. We have access to the right types of demographics you need to target, but this is a step reserved for once you are ready to spend money on marketing.

CONFIDENCE

Be confident even if you don't have houses to sell your buyers at the moment

Usually if you are upfront about your intentions with all things in life people will be willing to help you, especially if it does not impact them in a big way. Being upfront is a good policy to have, especially as a wholesaler. Transparency is a great way to build trust.

That may sound hypocritical, because I'm saying that a good way generate buyer leads is to put up for sale signs about the house that is not necessarily for sale. And to put up ads about a house that may not before sale, but let's be real here.

No one's getting hurt, and at the worst case you're wasting someone's time for one minute, while you get their email address. Your goal is the build a buyers list, and if you succeed, that one minute of their time can prove to be massively profitable for the both of you.

You'll be using scripts that we've worked on that have amazing success rates. Many times, these scripts will make you tell people that you have tons of houses available.

People would ask me almost daily, "Joe, do you have any homes for sale in this area?"

I'd always say yes, without even thinking about it. I say "yes, I have plenty. I have a ton for sale in that area. Send me a text with your email and I'll get the list over to you."

Think with the abundance mentality. You soon will have tons of houses. If you use the methods, I showed you, you'll be speaking nothing but the truth.

WORKING WITH ATTORNEYS AND TITLE COMPANIES

Look for a good attorney that gets work done quickly. Ask around for recommendations. You are looking for an attorney that frequently handles real estate transactions, namely the ones you are going to be starting with - wholesaling deals.

If the attorney you want to work with doesn't have experience working with wholesalers or doing double closings, ask them if they have any colleagues who do. You want to work with someone who knows how to make sure your deals close quickly, and correctly with minimal friction for you, your buyer, and seller.

Above all they need to know what your role in this deal is to ensure you get paid correctly. This leads into the next search to undergo looking for a title company.

Ask your attorney for recommendations for this as well, likely they will already have 1 or more title companies that they work closely with.

Call the title company and let them know that you are a local real estate investor and would like to see if they have experience working with wholesalers and assignable contracts or doing double closings.

Your main goal out of talking to them is to make sure that their company or your attorney will hold deposit checks in escrow for you and use the deposit you send to pay all or part of your "assignment fee".

The other method to close on a property is with a "double closing" or a "back to back closing". This isn't an ideal method for someone without much cash in the bank, because you will need to come out of pocket to buy the property, to in turn sell it to your end-buyer.

Ensure all your forms are fully legal and compliant for your jurisdiction. The best way to do this is to do a google search a figure out what regional real estate agent association has jurisdiction over your area.

In Florida, for example, it is rare to see an attorney overseeing a real estate closing. Everything is conducted at the title company. Do some research on who closes properties and which professionals are involved in a standard transaction in your area.

Another example, in Buffalo, NY, the regional association is the Buffalo Niagara Association of Real estate agents, or BNAR.

I'd do a google search for a BNAR Contract or I'd type out the full association name if that didn't produce anything.

Read the contract that you find, they can be lengthy and confusing. People turn their brains off when they read long and confusing things.

But there are certain parts of the contract that you are going to want to make sure are included or excluded.

Part of the service that we offer is personally consulting with you and guiding you through each deal that you make, to walk you through the doors of success.

Basically, you want to make sure that the contract is fully "assignable" and there's certain provisions that you want to add to every contract as "contingencies".

You may have to hand write it contingencies in a certain space on the contract with every deal that you make.

The purpose of using the regional contract is because you need to be able to take your contract to any lawyer in town to make sure that they can get this deal closed if you need them to.

Something and I found is that lawyers like to take vacation. If you only have one lawyer, you're going to find yourself being stuck one day.

And it's always good to lawyer shop so you know you aren't paying an inflated fee for this guy to sit on his ass for two weeks.

Ask these lawyers or title companies that you're calling if there are certain forms that are required for every single closing in your area or ask what the common forms are that they usually use with every closing.

Make sure to add or remove necessary forms to secure a smooth closing. Certain areas will require that the seller fill out a property condition disclosure, or a lead-based paint disclosure. Some areas the seller needs to disclose information about the property they know.

Here in NY, they need to fill out both. That's something that the title company or lawyer can help you with. They'll know the most common forms for your area.

You only have one impression with this buyer and seller, so make sure every form that will possibly be needed for this deal, is prepared, signed correctly and delivered to your lawyer in a timely manner.

You never want to have any preventable slowdowns in your closings. The burden here is largely placed on you, as the wholesaler and middleman of this transaction. Make sure the seller has all the correct legal forms signed. The form requirements may vary based on the jurisdiction you live in.

If you make sure that all parties have all necessary forms signed, you did all due diligence possible and got an adequate history from the seller - so no surprise judgements or liens pop up - then it should be a smooth closing.

Sometimes unforeseeable events do happen, and snags can delay a closing process, but if you did your part, your reputation as a reliable local wholesaler will remain intact. Word of mouth is everything here, so just make sure you pay attention to detail and get things done correctly. All professional parties involved will appreciate this and will gladly do business with you in the future.

SEARCH FOR SELLERS

There are many ways to find people who are selling their homes at wholesale prices. Sometimes they are really easy, most times, you need to do some work; and yes, you may even need to spend some money.

You are starting a business, so you need to be prepared to spend money to make money. If you are willing to trade time and effort, you will need to spend far less initially, if that is a concern.

That's the cost if you want to be your own boss in the end.

There really are a million ways to find sellers, finding off market deals is the only way to truly place yourself in an echelon above the other investors in your area.

Some databases I use cost me a monthly subscription fee, but most information is public record. If you are crafty enough, you can get all the info you need, to find people to sell you their property tomorrow - completely free.

Use social media to help track down the owner, use the county tax database websites. These are all free and easy tools that can help you get the job done.

WAYS TO FIND SELLERS

Like I mentioned before, some of these methods will cost money. But there are free methods. One free seller lead will turn into a deal that makes you thousands of dollars.

If you don't re-invest your profit into your marketing budget, you will never grow, and you will not have long term success.

All of these lead generation methods need to be employed at the same time. When it comes to finding sellers, you are using a shotgun and spraying and praying until you hit your targets. You're using a large net to catch a few prized fish.

Constantly look for new ways to find sellers, and dive deeper into the methods that are working well in your area. You can't catch anything if your net isn't in the water, and you can't catch anything if your net is too small.

Once the free methods find you some sellers, then transition into paid marketing techniques. Continue to employ all methods and constantly double down on each tactic every time they produce a worthy catch.

If you're catching a lot of fish you need to throw in some more nets, and some hooks too while you're at it.

CRAIGSLIST ADS

housing

apts / housing
housing swap
housing wanted
office / commercial
parking / storage
real estate for sale
rooms / shared
rooms wanted
sublets / temporary
vacation rentals

Craigslist is a massively utilized resource. This means two things, if you post an ad you can guarantee that a large audience will see the ad, but it also means that you have competition on any properties that are listed on here. Luckily, we can think creatively for many ways to use craigslist to find buyers and sellers.

Don't underestimate Craigslist. The site is actually one of the most technical websites behind the scenes. Don't post spammy type posts, and change up the way you write your ads when you start posting multiple posts.

If you don't you are going to get caught by their spam filter, and it just causes unnecessary delays.

Craigslist – For Sale

Property owners are going to be mainly found under the "housing" section on craigslist. You can start off your search in the most obvious part, by looking under the "real estate for sale" subsection.

Here you are going to find two different people, sellers and real estate agents. If you get in touch with a seller - perfect, you have a person who wants to sell and will probably be a buyer at some point in the future.

If you get in touch with an agent - most people would be discouraged. This is actually a great opportunity for you to network with someone who works in the local industry full time. They have their own buyers and sellers list, and if you know the right things to say, they'll give you access to their clientele.

They won't usually be very forthcoming with any information about their sellers or buyers if you ask directly. In fact, a lot of industry professionals are negative people for some reason.

Don't let negative people ruin your attitude when there are inbound and outbound business calls that you need to be ready to close. It doesn't make sense to carry around a chip on your shoulder from a 5 second interaction that went bad. Move on, Reset, and be ready for the next client.

We use specially prepared scripts that we follow exactly when we make outbound marketing calls to make sure we always close the deal.

You will probably run into wholesalers as well who post ads under this section, just like real estate agents, you can work with wholesalers to find good deals and sell them quickly.

Once you get in touch with a property owner on the FSBO section, you know that they are trying to sell, and you know they have a price in mind. Your job from here is honestly too easy.

If you have any difficulty, our mentors can guide your deal from any point in the process.

Craigslist - For Rent

A great way to find a property owner (a future seller) is to look under the "apt / housing" subsection of "housing".

Find the properties for rent and either give them a call or an email, or both.

For all of the investors that we contact we make sure we send out one of our hand-picked email templates, or we are using our specific voice call script to make sure we are asking the right questions to screen everyone into the right rolodex.

When you use the rental section, you are going to find landlords, who are real estate investors, and property managers.

Property managers are usually never going to give you any landlord info, in some cases it is their job to not do that.

When you talk to a property manager you are actually speaking to another real estate industry professional with a goldmine of a rolodex for you to tap into. You just need to know how to ask!

The "office / commercial and vacation rental sections may have some owners or property managers; you just need to check and ask. Many people with commercial portfolios may also have some residential property they want to sell.

Craigslist – Posting Ads

Post ads in various sections on Craigslist saying that you are looking to buy houses quickly and can make cash offers. Post them in the sections that are for garage sales, general for sale, general wanted sections – you get the idea.

There is a housing wanted section that is a good place to have a constant ad up. Post an aerial picture of your neighborhood or a google maps screenshot

You always want a picture on your craigslist posts, so you show up in more search results.

If the ad is free to post – post a few different variations in a few different sections. Sometimes craigslist will make you pay $5 to post an ad.

Definitely post in these sections! You can guarantee that your ad will be getting looked at by a large number of people.

Remember, people who buy also sell, and it is always a great idea to continually build a list of people who are actively looking to buy. You can post ads under the "real estate for sale by owner" section.

Make an ad about a property using our template so you can guarantee that investors will want to buy it. Soon you will start getting phone calls.

Use our script so you can evaluate your buyers to see if they are also selling any property.

PUBLIC RECORDS WEBSITES

There are many public records websites where you can look up property owner information. In most cases the websites are all very easy to use. With practice you can get an owner mailing address and phone number in a matter of minutes, and you can be talking to them about selling you their house that much sooner.

My way off the ground when I first started was that I was that I was a licensed real estate agent. My thousands of dollars of real estate association dues also gave me access to their public records website.

Through that website, real estate agents are able to run public records searches, looking through tax information to find property owner information. They can then export this data into an excel file with all of the info neatly arranged in columns.

There are a few ways to get access to this information:

- Use a paid service for $80-125 per month.
- Ask a real estate agent to send you this information – pay for it if needed!

If you are a student under our mentorship, use the programs we give you access to and you can quickly "skip trace" the owners of any property and export your targeted list of owner data into an excel file.

One decent 3rd party company that allows access to a wide variety of tools is "realeflow". This company allows you to do search for owners of property in your area and export up to 5,000 public records in an excel file.

Once I do these searches, I will skip trace the owners and get their information. If the phone number is not a good number or if I am doing a mailing campaign, I'll filter the list of all the owner information to the people I want to mail letters to.

Once I have a big list of names and addresses, I will target these homes and send them a specially designed letter that almost always gets a response.

From there we can move forward and make a deal happen with everyone's interests aligned.

Some of the people I target (the people who catch my eye) when I am doing searches:

Absentee owners

These may be listed as "non owner occupied" property. This means that the owner of the house has a different mailing address than the property.

This is a real estate investor. If you have the ability, try to search for their name directly, you will most likely see that they own many properties - and they're for sale for the right price.

LLC owners

Anyone who lists their ownership as an LLC, or INC, or some sort of legal entity. These people are investors who are probably a little savvier than the average investor. They don't want their name out there in public record, and they don't want to expose themselves to any unnecessary liability. These are investors who also have property for sale.

Same owner multiple houses

If you see the same name coming up while scrolling through the MLS or some public records website, you should search for their name directly. Odds are you will see their extensive list of property they own, and you can give them a call and see about their interest in selling

Probates

These owners have died, and have left their property to their relatives, or the ownership is questionable.

Most cases the relatives don't want anything to do with the property, and they usually are very happy if someone will come in to buy the home, so they don't need to deal with the mortgage company.

Usually we need to get this list from the city or call attorneys to see if they have any properties that we could potentially purchase from the relatives.

MAILING CAMPAIGNS

Once you do a public records search and obtain owner information you have everything you need for a direct mail marketing campaign.

If you target any one or more of the groups above, you will get a great response with mailing or phone campaigns. We usually reserve sending letters out for the people that we couldn't get in touch with on the phone. That's mainly because its much quicker to call someone than to wait for mail.

Like I said before, you should already have public record data exported. The information you need are the Owner name, and their full tax billing address. The place that their tax bill gets sent is usually a place that you can reach them with letters that you send.

Use our letter template and use the "mail merge" feature to make custom letters with the property owner names plugged in the correct places.

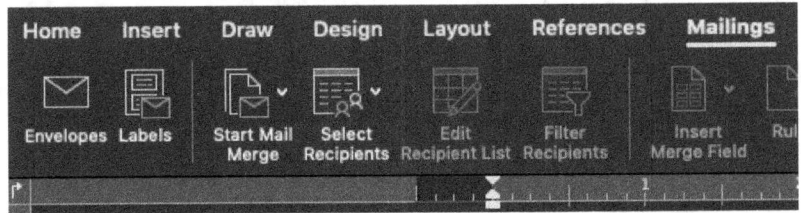

Google how to perform this function on Microsoft word or google docs, it is a very effective tool to make highly professional mailing campaigns.

You can also use mail merge to print labels to stick to envelopes or print directly on the envelope. Printing directly on the envelope can help you save money and time buying and sticking labels on each outgoing letter.

We also like to use "un-ruled" (meaning the ones without the lines) neon 4x6 index cards and print post card templates directly on the front and back. This is the cheapest method to mail, because all you need is printer ink, index cards, and stamps.

A few days after you drop your letters in the mail you should start getting phone calls from your sellers, looking to show you their property they have available.

The more appealing your letter, the more likely it will get opened. The better the content of your letter, the more likely you will get a phone call in return.

You can target a quarter mile radius and spend anywhere from $100-300 on mailing letters. I would say this is a good starting point to fine tune your target areas and demographics for your mailing campaigns.

We print red font on loose-leaf paper and even developed our own font to make the letters look hand-written.

> Dear <name>,
>
> My name is Joe Coello and I want to buy your property at <address>.
>
> If you are interested in <u>selling</u> please call me at (321) 266-7256.
>
> I can act quickly with no <u>drawn out</u> process. I will buy your property in "AS-IS" condition.
>
> Please call anytime.
> Respectfully,
> Joe Coello
> (321) 266-7256
>
> P.S. I'm wanting to buy soon, please call.

Using un-lined 4x6 neon note cards is a cheap way to make your own postcards. Postcard stamps are cheaper than regular first-class stamps, so you can get more houses per mailing campaign if money is an issue starting out.

Larkspur York
28 York St
Suite 1
Buffalo, NY 14213

Place Postage Here

Larkspur York
R E A L   E S T A T E

We Want to Make You a Cash Offer on Your Home!

<Owner name>

<address>

Hello <Owner Name>,

My name is McKenzie Potter and I want to buy your house at <address>.

If you have any interest in selling, I can make you a CASH offer to quickly buy your house AS-IS!

    Please give me a call at (716) 202-0662
    or email at mckenzie@Larkspuryork.com

Thank you.
McKenzie

    P.S. I want to buy soon please call me!

DRIVING STREETS

The industry term for this is also called "driving for dollars." This is a great method to get yourself a ton of leads.

Make sure you leave the house with your business cards, some pens, a notepad and a general idea of the area of where you are going to be driving around.

We also use a hand-written note template and print out hundreds of copies. We leave these notes on people's door when they don't answer.

Look for "For Sale by Owner" signs, "For Sale" and "For Rent" signs in your target neighborhood.

Signs from a real estate agent means that this current house is not available to you until the "agency" agreement expires between the real estate agent and the seller. Sometimes there is the rare occasion where the real estate agent does not have exclusive agency with the seller, so you can still wholesale the property.

Mark down the addresses of the houses that have signs and give them a call. Sometimes they will be at the house so you can get right in there and start looking around. Use every opportunity and every phone call as a chance for you to build rapport.

Go up to the doors and knock and use our script to talk to the resident/owner. Once you get more experience, you will start to learn what houses are the best ones to target.

The ugliest home on the best block, or the home that needs work. Those are the ones that we usually go up to and knock on the door and leave notes for.

If they answer the door, introduce yourself and see if they are motivated sellers or not. If they are the owner of the property make sure you leave them with your business card and let them know to hold on to it if they ever think their circumstances may change to where they would be interested in taking an all cash offer to buy their house as-is.

You can also opt to call all of them at once when you get back to your home/office. Use our script to either get them in your rolodex as a buyer, or to add them to your list of properties that you need to conduct due diligence on.

FSBO WEBSITES

FSBO means "For Sale by Owner". There are many websites that cater to the everyday American who wants to buy a home or sell their home. Let's just focus our time on the sites that get the most traffic.

This is going to change from time to time, and it will also change based on where you live. I recommend doing a google search for "For sale by owner"

The pages that are ranked higher, get more traffic. So, pick the top 3-4 sites and focus there.

What we do with these sites are both post the homes that we get under contract, and other homes we have for sale.

To find sellers here we simply contact the people who are selling their homes.

These are most likely off-market property, because if they had an agreement with most real estate agents, the owner couldn't sell the home themselves without the agent getting a cut.

Zillow, Trulia, Redfin, and a few other sites with variations of "for sale by owner.com" - These generally get the most traffic. So, focus your effort here. Most people looking to buy are going to mainly see the home on Zillow or Redfin anyway.

We're going to just focus on Zillow for now. So, go to Zillow and type in the city you are in. Then use the draw tool on the map to select the area you want to search in.

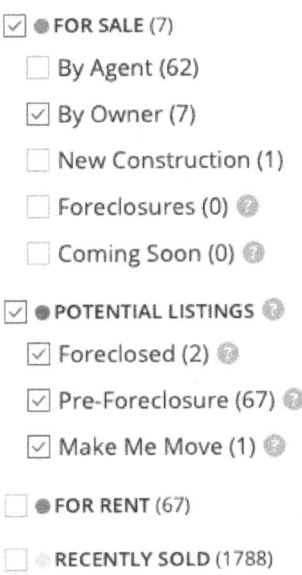

When you are looking for sellers, select the boxes you see above.

Sometimes, I de-select the pre-foreclosure box because that usually has more results than the other categories combined.

If their home isn't under this category, the home is most likely being listed by a real estate agent. This isn't useful if you are directly looking for a seller to get under contract. But there is definitely some utility in knowing some local real estate agents.

Make sure all the other search filters fit within your parameters. Clear out all the other filters if you are un-sure what to look for.

Once you select a property, pay close attention.

Zillow will hide the owner information, usually at the bottom of the page.

For sale by owner listings will have the owner information at the very bottom in a bracket that looks like this:

Listing provided by owner

Usually under this, there will be a phone number.

For the pre-foreclosure and foreclosure listings, you will see columns like these:

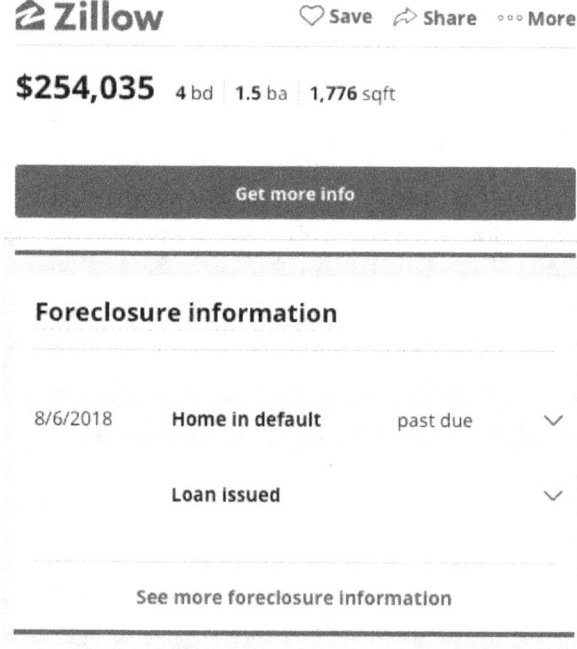

Click the "see more foreclosure information" tab

Foreclosure Trustee or Attorney

Name:

Address:

Phone:

Legal

Foreclosure type: Judicial

Recorded: Notice of Lis Pendens on 8/7/2018

Parcel number: 140200 100.22-3-22

Learn more at Zillow Foreclosure Center

Here you will see the attorney information, who you can call you try and get more information about the property.

The best thing to really do in this situation is to go to the house and leave a note on the door, and try to find the owner's email and phone number from a skip tracing company.

These homeowners are distressed in some way for their mortgage company to have filed a pre-foreclosure notice.

It may be possible that a cash offer may help to solve their problem.

I will basically tell them in person or on the phone, how my company can help fix and remove the burden associated with this property.

When you approach homeowners with the mentality that you are trying to solve their problem that they have with their home, you can often times find the best solution for both you and them.

Some other great sellers to buy from are on Zillow are under the "make me move" category. When you click on one of those houses, look at the column to the right. We have a screenshot of what it looks like below.

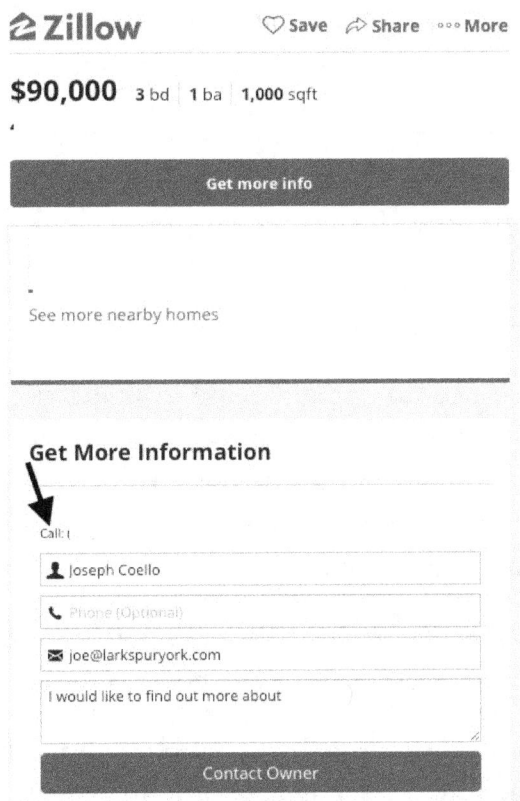

This contact information is hidden in a contact block. I dropped an arrow in the picture above where you can usually find the owner phone number for these types if listings.

These numerous types of listings should provide you with plenty of leads from Zillow, Trulia, and other similar sites.

Always remember to ask the sellers if they have other properties available.

Don't waste your time trying to get into contact with people who have newly renovated homes posted on these sites. They will want top dollar for their home, and these types of property are not ideal candidates to wholesale.

They are however great people to add to your buyers list – especially if they are flipping and renovating a lot of houses in the area.

AUCTIONS

You will have to do some digging to figure out when and where the local real estate auctions are in your area. They are usually run by the county or the city, so calling the housing department, or the tax appraiser is probably a safe place to start your search.

Once you get the information about all the different property auctions in your area – show up to one of them.

You aren't necessarily a buyer of any property, but the people who are at these auctions are usually investors themselves. Be social and have some business cards to hand out.

Make conversation and build rapport with people who attend and ask around if anyone is selling any property.

You already know they are buying property – so collect business cards and save everyone's contact info for your buyer's list as well.

SOCIAL MEDIA

There is a method to find buyers and sellers on every social media platform. If you can be creative, you can find yourself an endless inventory of buyers and sellers on the internet.

Facebook

One of the largest, if not currently the largest social media platform around. Facebook is one of the best methods for finding highly motivated sellers.

You should have already been following my methods for finding buyers above.

If you have, then you are already in the correct groups you need to be in.

You need to join groups for garage sales, for clubs, local activity and sales groups. Join the biggest local groups that you can join. Barter, yard sales, and groups of that nature have really provided me a ton of quality leads in the past.

Once you are in a group, make a post for each group.

"I want to buy your home! I'm a cash buyer looking for a property in <city> area. I want single family or multi-family. I can close quickly (555) 555-5555"

Use similar variations of that post and send it out across your groups. Renew the postings often and be ready to be able to see the homes quickly. You should get a great response from here.

You can also use the search function at the top of the page and use alternating phrases with keywords that people would include if they were selling a home.

"Philadelphia duplex" or "Orlando house for sale" as a search string in Facebook will bring up all the posts that are viewable to you with all of those keywords in it.

You should see several people, in public groups, or the private groups you are a member in – that are selling their homes. Send them a message on Facebook or call them if they list their phone number.

These are two great methods to find seller leads on Facebook.

If you get creative you can utilize Facebook to find plenty of homeowners and sellers who you can help by making a cash offer on their home and re-selling the contract.

When you make money from free leads, set aside a portion of your profit to spend on paid marketing methods. This will guarantee that you continue to find deals and never stagnate.

LinkedIn

LinkedIn is a great networking platform. You should have a network of at least 1,000 real estate connections within a few weeks if you have been following my advice.

From there LinkedIn makes it very easy to export the email address of your connections in an excel file. You can find many guides how to do this step by step if you google it.

This most likely won't be very fruitful for you because most people won't opt for their info to be exported. If they did then that is great!

If you are like me and many others, many of your connections on LinkedIn make it a little more difficult to contact them.

We use special programs to help find the contact info of our connections on LinkedIn, but if you don't have access to these types of programs you can still get the email and phone numbers you need!

It will take a little longer, but that's ok, because each lead will be a direct connection.

Select one of your connections on LinkedIn and scroll all the way down on their page. You should see a column that lists their email address and their phone number. It will definitely at least have one of these filled out.

Use an email that we designed or that you designed to introduce yourself and ask if they have any properties they are interested in selling. I recommend giving them a message on LinkedIn first, then phone call (leave a voicemail), and then sending an email to follow up.

REAL ESTATE INVESTOR MEETUPS

Meetups, Conferences, and seminars are great places to find buyers and sellers. You should be getting used to acting like a social butterfly by now, so take advantage of these networking events to expand your rolodex.

Get your name out there and remember to tell everyone you run into that "I'm a real estate investor. I buy and sell houses."

There are plenty of apps, websites and networking groups that are designed for real estate investors. If you don't take advantage of them, you are losing a great resource to another wholesaler in your area who has more hunger for it than you.

Anytime you are somewhere new, talk about real estate to the point of annoyance to those close to you. That's the level you should be at if you are serious about success in this competitive industry.

VIOLATIONS LIST

Township Building Inspectors go around the city and make sure that each property is up to code. Depending on the area you are in, the requirements may be more or less strict.

Either case, the list of houses that have violations against them are public information. If you call your cities housing department you will be able to find someone who can help you put a request in to view the list of homes with active violations against them.

A Freedom of Information Act or FOIA request is often necessary to attain these documents.

Once you have the list of property, and owners you can start to work to contact them and see if they are willing to sell their property.

For obvious reasons you can see that this niche of sellers may be extra motivated to sell their property.

INDUSTRY PROFESSIONALS

People who work in Real Estate full time have a large network of other people in the industry. It is a great practice to start contacting these professionals and start building rapport with them. The larger your network is the more money you will directly make in Real Estate.

Real estate agents and property managers fall into these categories. They often times have off market properties or know of them, or they know people who would be willing to buy the deals you have.

Money talks and bullshit walks. Offer them a finders fee, commission, or consulting fee for their troubles or to incentivize them to bring you a deal in the future. Follow up every couple of weeks just to shoot the breeze and build rapport to really reap the rewards of relationships like these. Anything from private hard money lender connections to numerous wholesale deals can result from it.

Attorneys

Attorneys are the gatekeepers to many aspects of real estate deals depending on the state you are in. They have huge networks of buyers and sellers.

Attorneys handle great deals all the time like:

- Pre-foreclosures
- Foreclosures
- Probates
- Divorces

They also handle closings and work with investors and wholesalers. If you know the right questions to ask, you can get all the information you need to find great property to wholesale or buy for yourself.

Call up a family planning or estate lawyer and ask them if they have any clients who your company could assist with a cash offer.

I often will call up a lawyer I haven't worked with before and say "Hey my name is Joe from Larkspur York Real Estate. We're a real estate investment company in the area and I was just calling to see if you had any clients who would be interested in a cash offer for their property. We buy all property types, and we buy them as-is."

My students and independent contractors who work under the Larkspur York umbrella say similar things on the phone and we often see a great result from lawyers who are happy to have a legitimate company help their solve client's issues.

Section 8 housing lists

Section-8 is a public assistance program that is available in many regions of the nation. The government won't pay for any house to be rented; they must conduct inspections on all houses that are qualified to accept section-8.

Landlords who accept section 8 tenants often apply to put their houses on the housing list so they can find tenants easier.

Social workers and other public housing / non-profit housing companies also fit in this category.

Give them a call and see if you can get ahold of the housing list, or list of approved landlords. It might take a trip to the office, but you will have a roster of a few hundred investors who are willing to buy or sell.

Title Companies

Title companies may in some cases, act as the sole party handling a closing depending on the area you are in.

These companies are often just as essential as a lawyer. They also have a large roster of contacts that you may be able to connect with if you approach the topic delicately.

Call around to your local title companies and explain to them that you are looking to buy property and if they know of any local investors that are selling any property off market.

If they are having a good day, and if you build some rapport on the phone call, they might put you in touch with some investors with some property to sell.

Property managers

Property managers work with people that own one or more properties. These owners may not be willing to sell the property they have under management, but they may have multiple other properties they are willing to sell.

In my experience, I have seen numerous property managers that know about off-market deals. They are most likely managing some rentals that they know need too much work for their current client to repair. They are usually aware somewhat about the financial status of their clients and which properties are best for them to get rid of.

Offer them a commission for any leads they bring you and most of them will start emailing you over portfolios you can start wholesaling.

Use our script to call a property management company and they will help guide you towards homes or investors they know who some property may have they want to part ways with.

Real estate agents & Wholesalers

Other people professionally working in the same capacity as you, also have the same network as you, or larger.

Odds are, since mostly everyone has been doing it longer than you at this point, they all have bigger networks. Befriending other people who work as Agents or who wholesale properties is always a great idea.

If you call any for sale sign with an MLS logo or any "we buy houses" bandit sign you can get in touch with either a Real Estate Salesperson / Agent / Real estate agent or a fellow Wholesaler.

If you send any Real estate agent, Wholesaler, Lawyer, Title Company or Property Manager a property, try to get access to some of their sellers in return. Tell them about open houses you may have and network with everyone you see.

Like with any part of the real estate business, and most other industries: money talks and bullshit walks. If you are in a position to give these guys a small tip, maybe $100-200, and let them know. "Hey I don't want you to work for free – but if you know of any off market deals, send em my way."

On top of that – I offer wholesalers and agents 5-10% commission if they send me any off-market properties. Make sure you pay people who bring you deals and the word will get around. These industry professionals can keep you busy.

MAKE EDUCATED OFFERS – INTRO TO A CMA

This step is going to be really confusing if you don't know where to start. Making an offer on a property is a daunting task if you don't know how to get the right information.

You need to know how much money homes cost in the areas that you are targeting. This is what you need to develop an expertise in. It will be a huge factor on if you will be a successful wholesaler or not.

If you don't have access to the MLS then determining the price a home should cost may be hard, but it's not impossible. Usually you can get enough information through Zillow to get yourself in a pretty narrow range.

Plug in your city in Zillow and search for homes that are for sale and that have already sold.

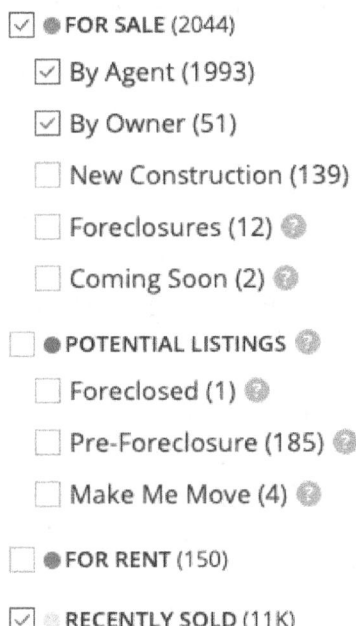

Tip: don't ignore the "Zestimate"

The Zestimate is definitely not a good way to determine the property value – BUT – it is what the average consumer looks at.

Since 95% of the people who you will be buying from, and selling to – are putting weight into this number – you should pay attention to it.

You can use this many times to make cash offers on properties at tens of thousands of dollars below their market value because Zillow has the zestimate which is very far from correct price.

I can't count how many times Zillow has totally incorrect information about a property:

- The wrong number of bedrooms
- Wrong square footage
- Etc.

Use this to your advantage so you can buy low and sell high.

Sometimes the zestimate is much higher than what the property is actually worth. Just educate the owner why their property is actually worth much less than what Zillow says.

Use accurate comparative properties (comps) to validate what you say.

COMPARATIVE MARKET ANALYSIS (CMA)

Essentially what you need to do for every property is something called a comparative market analysis. Real estate agents will call this is CMA.

When I would do commercial and residential valuations for the banks and mortgage companies, I would often do a lot of CMAs in many different areas on many different property types.

You really need to do a lot of them before you start understanding how pricing works in your local area.

But the basics are that you are looking at all of the properties in the area that are similar to your subject property, in other words the property that you are looking at wholesaling.

You're looking at the recent sales in the past year, in addition to all of the homes that are on the market and all the homes that are under contract. But only the ones that are similar to the deal you have.

Search Filters

The criteria that need to remain the same are the number of bedrooms, number of bathrooms. The number of garage spaces and the type a garage like if it's detached or attached.

If there's a pool or not, or if the property is waterfront riverfront lakefront anything like that anything special about the property should be taken into consideration of possible.

Try to also search for homes with the same type of basement or crawlspace if applicable, like if the basement is finished or if it's a full basement, or if there's no basement at all.

The variable information is going to be the square footage. So, search for properties about 200 ft.² smaller and 200 ft.² bigger than your subject property. For example, if you have a property that is thousand square feet, your search would be any home between 800 and 1200 ft.²

Do the same range for the lot size.

If you live in a very densely populated city then you're only going to be using a quarter mile radius from your subject property.

If you're in a smaller city or the suburbs you can expand it to a half mile radius.

If you're in a rural area then you can use a one-mile radius, try to stay under 5 miles.

You should be able to do a search for many of these properties on Zillow or other sites like that, at least show you the homes that are currently listed.

Real estate agents have access to search indexes that are specially formatted to allow them to quickly do CMA's on any property in their region.

Doing a CMA is the best way to determine the price of a property and what the after-repair value (ARV) is.

ARV

The ARV is the price you can make when you sell your home on the open market after all repairs are made. The "open market" the way that I'm saying it, refers to property that is listed by a real estate agent on the multiple listing service or MLS.

If a home is listed on the MLS that means a Real estate agent has an "Agency agreement" signed with that owner. Oftentimes, this agency agreement gives the Real estate agent exclusive agency, meaning that if the home sells, even if the owner finds a buyer and the real estate agent does nothing, the real estate agent still gets their guaranteed commission.

Pulling Comps

After you run this search you will see a list of homes that broadly fit the characteristics of your subject property. Do a quick check on the range of prices, they could be a narrow or a wide range of prices.

From there you need to further narrow the list based on the condition and quality of the homes. You can do this by looking at the exterior pictures and google street view photos of all the comparable properties compared to the subject property.

The higher quality and newly renovated homes reflect the ARV of the subject property. The homes that look about equal in condition reflect the current asking price.

You need to look at the homes that actually sold to see the actual value of the properties, but looking at the list price and the average days on market for some of the properties in the same area as you will give you an indication as to how valuable your property is.

Try to find at least 3 comparable properties that are actively listed and 3 that have sold.

That will give you a good range of prices to narrow down an estimation of price and get you in the ballpark for now.

This is definitely a very important and crucial step to making sure you profit in this business.

You don't want to be making offers that give you little profit or miss out on profit by offering too high and accepting too little.

If you are having trouble doing a CMA just give us an email or a call. We want wholesalers who use the Larkspur York brand to have all the tools available to them to succeed.

QUICKLY ESTIMATING REPAIRS

After you get the value of the home in good condition or possibly the current condition, you need to estimate the cost of repairs.

When you look through the home take note of the floors, ceilings and walls. Look for signs of water damage, cracking, discoloration, warping etc.

Look at the quality and condition of all of those items. Annotate if they need replacement.

The best way to document this type of stuff is by taking pictures and video. Try to include entire rooms with your pictures and take the best pictures you can.

You will need some pictures to show future investors, so make sure the lighting is good.

Don't ever assume it will be easy to get back into a property, even if everyone seems friendly. Get good pictures so you won't have to return as much, or only when necessary.

When you look at a room that is ugly, or needs renovations, you see a disgusting place that you want to run out of. The best wholesalers will instead see dollar signs.

They're finding the ugliest house on the best block, and wholesaling to a flipper who will buy it and give them a $10,000 assignment fee.

The ability to estimate repairs is so crucial in determining the overall value of the home. You should be looking at all the real estate hashtags on Facebook and Instagram and getting a sense of what the current style is for your area.

There is most likely a popular type of bathroom, certain colors, certain furnishings that will make a home on the market sell for more money and quicker.

The further away your subject property is from that standard, the further it is from the ARV or after repair value.

The materials that you use further repairs will be highly dependent on the neighborhood that you're in.

You're not going to be using $10 per square foot tile in the house that will only be worth $90,000 when its fully repaired.

That kind of a house is most likely going to be getting flooring that costs one dollar per square foot.

If you need to quickly get a rough estimate of repairs immediately, I would go off these guidelines:

- Minor repairs: can be estimated at $5 per square foot
- Moderate repairs: can be estimated at $15 per square foot

- Total renovations: can be estimated at $20 per square foot

This is a picture of a wall at a property I just assigned to an end buyer, for a $12,750 assignment fee.

How much would you estimate the repairs on that wall to cost?

You should be quoting everyone the cost that a contractor would most likely charge. If you are very unsure you can call a contractor to come in with you, or maybe bring a friend who works in this line of work.

They may be able to help you determine the costs involved. They will vary slightly based on the region you live in.

Repairing this wall doesn't take much, some drywall tape, mud and paint and it will look brand new.

I would categorize the repairs needed for this type of situation as minor. I would only recommend attempting to repair something like this yourself, if you have experience doing drywall and painting. If you aren't an expert, don't mess with it.

The flipper you are selling it to will have an expert do the repair. The people who want to live in the home ultimately will appreciate that.

This is a picture of the bathroom in the same property.

This is still something in the minor category.

Most homes will have a mix of area needing a range of repairs from minor, up to major.

Major repairs are on par with totally gutting a house to the studs and redoing everything.

The more specialties that are involved with a repair the more expensive the repair. General Contractors can sub contract to all of them: Plumbers, electricians, architects, whoever is needed for a job.

Any big-ticket item is going to be an additional cost as well. Things like:

- Roof

- Structural Repair (Foundation/ Framing / exterior brick repair)
- HVAC (AC, Boiler or Furnace replacement/repair)
- Water and Plumbing line repairs
- Electric line or circuit breaker repairs/updates
- Septic/sewer issues

Things like bathroom and kitchen renovations can range from $5,000-$20,000 per room. If the siding or windows need to be replaced, those are also several thousand-dollar items.

Take every aspect into account when you are accounting for repairs.

If the math makes sense to you, it will make sense to a flipper.

What is a Good Deal?

Purchase Price + Repairs = (Several Thousand Less than ARV)

The cheaper the purchase price, the cheaper the repairs, and the higher the ARV – the more profit there is to be made.

Leave plenty of room for a flipper to make $20,000-40,000 and you can take the difference as your assignment fee.

Flippers will sell their property after they fix it up, for the full market value. That means they will usually aim to get the full ARV.

How does a flipper do their math? Basically, like this:

ARV - (Repairs) - (Purchase Price) = Profit

If there is room for you to take a modest profit, and for the flipper to make their profit, you should move on the deal — or make an offer at a price that will give you your target profit.

GETTING YOUR OFFER ACCEPTED

Knowing the right things to say and when are crucial to closing any deal, especially the ones in real estate.

The best way to ensure you close the deal is to use a script. If you are under our mentorship you already have full access and permission to use all of the scripts I use to get sellers to accept my offer and sign my assignable contract so I can wholesale their property – as well as the ability to use the Larkspur York brand to make cash offers.

Included will also be all of the scripts I use to build my buyers list, my scripts to find sellers, and my scripts to find buyers and sellers from attorneys, title companies, property managers and real estate agents.

I even have scripts to find off market deals, tax lien properties, foreclosures, judgements, and housing violations.

All of these property owners will sell you their property if you know the right things to ask, and the properly timed and expert crafted responses.

You need to be able to assess what type of contract to use, because each situation is different.

You also need to be able to know what types of contingencies to write into your contract to ensure that you minimize your risk and increase your profit.

WHAT SHOULD I SAY?

A good salesperson has a lot of things to say to clients to overcome objections, and to get people to agree to their price.

A great salesperson knows when to utilize these lines, and keeps them in their back pocket, in their toolbox for when the right one is needed.

Ask difficult questions, and ask the questions you need to know to do your job easier:

How much do you owe on this property?

Do you have a real number or estimation on how much this property needs in repair?

What do you want to get for this home, like really, what is the lowest price you'll be happy taking? – and please don't break my back man, I gotta make a small profit after I do all this work and spend all that money over the next 3 months.

I talk to people like they are my friend from back home. I say "Hey man, what is the realistic price you are willing to come to on this property?" then I stay silent and maintain eye contact until they say something.

Rarely will people come back to you initially with a price. Often a common response is "I don't know right now I'll have to talk to my wife (or do more research) and get back to you" another common one is "Well I want you to make me an offer"

Never say the price first or say the first number – always make them say their first number.

Reply to this by sticking to your guns and cycling through the same 3 lines:

"I know you do but I gotta hear what the lowest you will take is"

"Yeah I hear you, but c'mon man what's a realistic number on this one"

"Haha I get it, but in actuality I gotta know, what is a good number that we can make a deal on?"

Add some variation and seem human. Be lighthearted and smile and laugh about it. If you get too serious, and aggression is the tone in the air, you won't make a fruitful deal.

Really make sure you harp on all of the little deficiencies you need to upgrade. Do they have new laminate counter? Say Yeah but still we'll have to re-do it to get the highest price, the standard for the market value in the area is really only granite or formica.

Find anything and everything negative to talk about in regards to why their home needs to be reduced in price. Be creative - offer your additional move out coordination services or whatever else the homeowner needs to get the deal closed.

CONTINGENCIES AND OTHER TYPES OF CONTRACTS

A contingency is a clause in a contract that allows either party to have special privileges.

If you are wholetailing your contract needs to include a contingency allowing for you to take possession of the property and make certain specific improvements.

Over time you'll become more comfortable with your contracts and getting deals structured and closed. It takes times to learn about different types of contracts and the best contingencies to include in your deals.

A different type of contract may be best in certain situations, but it takes some knowledge and experience to know when to use which tool for which job. We don't expect you to know how to set deals like this up, which is why we have an open door policy so you can come to use before the ball gets dropped and the deal dies.

For example:

If they don't want to sell their home but will instead let you rent it, Lease option contracts are a way to give you the option to purchase the property at a set purchase price at the end of, or during the lease term.

Basically, what you are doing is getting the seller to sign the rights of the house over to you via lease option contract. This allows you to do things like, clean outs or painting, all depending on the certain property situation.

Not only do you need to know about other types of contracts – you need to be an expert on the contract that you are using to wholesale with. You need to read it and re-read it to understand what they mean sometimes.

Look at all the boxes that can be checked, and all the places that can be initialed and signed. Look at what it means if they are or aren't signed.

I included some contingencies that we use. Excuse my terrible handwriting, but it shows you that each deal is different and how flexible you need to be with being able to amend a contract.

I don't use cookie cutter contingencies for every seller. Sometimes, adding un-necessary clauses only makes the seller less likely to deal with you.

20. **OTHER TERMS.** *(If blank, this paragraph is not applicable.)* In the event of a conflict between the provisions of this paragraph and the provisions of any other paragraph of this Contract, the provisions of this paragraph shall control.
1. Seller must pay off mortgage so title may be transferred.
2. Buyer will pay for Seller's closing costs.
3. Title search will be 40 year search
4. One member of the LLC is a licensed Agent in NYS

Some contingencies that are nice to have:

- Seller must pay off all liens and clear all violations prior to closing
- Title Search will be a 40-year search

- Contract contingent upon Buyer's inspection and approval of the property prior to transfer of title.

- Seller agrees to provide access to Buyer's representatives prior to transfer of title for inspection, and to market the property.

- Subject to approval of financing by mortgage company.

HARD TO CLOSE SELLERS

Wholesaling is one of the toughest "jobs" in real estate because you need to be great in almost every aspect of the transaction (marketing, analysis, communication, sales, negotiation, etc.), but it is constantly taught as an entry level skill by the "gurus" of real estate.

Sometimes it can be hard to convince a seller to work with you as a wholesaler, especially if you are a new wholesaler. When you're being presented with a seller who is not very receptive to your sales pitch, it is very important to slow it down and listen to what they are saying.

There is absolutely no reason why the seller, the end buyer, and you, the wholesaler, don't walk away from every deal feeling satisfied with their outcome. Are you approaching this situation with the mindset that you were solving someone's problem?

Yes, you can and will make between $2000, $5000, and even $10,000 or more from assigning contracts. So, money can be a distracting factor, but that does not mean that you need to take advantage of people or be unethical.

If you just listen to the property owner and listen to their problems, you can find out the motivations they may have to sell their property.

There are many techniques that you can use and there are many methods that people recommend. When it comes to wholesaling it can be very simple, as long as you do one important thing.

You must earn the property owners trust. For everyone on your buyers list and for every prospective seller – you need to have the mindset that your goal is to provide them the best outcome for their situation.

If you are having issues talking to sellers, or closing deals, you need to be self-aware and do an accurate, and harsh self-assessment.

First of all, are you using and good sales pitch? If you are just free styling it especially during your first deals, you're just setting yourself up for failure. You need to come off as polished and your sales pitch needs to be refined, your authority in this field is going to be what is the difference between a seller walking and you closing a sale and taking home a $5000 assignment fee.

Did you know that hospitals that have surgical checklist in plain view have drastically less rates of accidents? Coming from a background as an Army medic, I'm very used to reviewing protocols and doing pre-Mission inspections to make sure that everything from the bullets to the Band-Aids were ready to go.

It's no different than a hospital checking its crash cart before every shift or a businessman making sure there fully prepared for the next presentation. We always review our script with a fine-tooth comb before we approach a seller whether on the phone or in person.

Self-awareness is also key. You need to be fully aware of how you come off to other people. People will judge a book by its cover, and you will be judged by your appearance. How you look, how you sound, the clothes you wear, your haircut, your personal hygiene, all of it. Present yourself professionally and you will be received professionally.

Being the self-aware wholesaler that you are, you need to remember that you do not want to come off as too pushy, if you break your trust or lose trust it is much harder to regain it any close the deal.

Even though It's not impossible, because a great real estate investor is also persistent and knows that when a seller says "no" it just means not right now. You can always send them a letter in a week or give them a call back to see if they change their mind.

But naturally still, because wholesaling is not a real estate method that falls within the norm, many sellers will be very hesitant to work with you. You need to listen to their objections and take notes so that you can be prepared to respond to them in a way that allows them to place their trust in you.

Being an empathetic and socially aware wholesaler is going to guarantee that you will be able to make more than one deal in this business.

Walking away is one of the biggest negotiation tools that you can use. Remember that there's always another deal, do not fall victim to the scarcity mindset. Besides, if you are following the methods that we are showing you to get leads and find sellers then you should already have an overflowing funnel of deals.

Over the years we have heard many reasons that property owners have told us, why they will not work with us....at first.

We have developed an algorithm that we use in practice with so that we can quickly respond to 99% of the hesitations that a seller may have. While you can get our multiple deal algorithms, I'll show you some of the biggest selling points that you can use to help close the deal with your seller.

WHY SHOULD THEY WORK WITH YOU?

One of the biggest reasons that a seller would want to work with the wholesaler is that we can boast an extensive network of cash buyers/partners who are willing to buy their house yesterday. This is our list of investors that we worked hard to get. And that's why they are better serving themselves by working with you. But above all, let your seller know that you can close on their house fast.

Also make sure that you reiterate to them that they are going to get paid in cash on closing – with no hassle for any banks or mortgages and no time needed for checks to clear.

Some of the more negative people in real estate say that wholesalers are basically scumbags. They say the wholesalers are untrustworthy, I mean why would you work with one? Especially when you can just work with the licensed real estate agent?

Well, I am a licensed real estate agent, and I still wholesale properties – and the seller makes more money at the end of the day in most cases.

How does this work? Because when you wholesale a property, the deal is completely off market. This means that no broker and no agent need to split commissions or take any commissions out.

In a typical real estate transaction that hits the market, the seller is going to pay the selling side broker, the selling side agent, the buyer side broker, and the buyer side agent. Typically, this is all taken out in one big chunk, this is called the commission.

I'll tell you right now they say that there's no industry standard and that price-fixing is illegal but usually you're going to see between five and 6% commission. That means that, if I were to list your home today, I get 6% of the sales price of the home if I found the buyer as well.

If I buy your home as a wholesaler, I'm not acting as a real estate agent, so you pay no commissions. The buyer pays that end when the deal is kept off market.

Why don't all sellers keep their homes off market then?

Because it's hard, and because it's YOUR job to procure and maintain that network of buyers & sellers.

This becomes an even bigger selling point if you set your eyes on the larger price tag properties. If you display confidence that you can do what you say, people have no reason not to believe you. Only when you stop following through on your word, does it become an issue.

If you find end buyers for those properties, and take a modest assignment fee for yourself, most times it will still be far less than the commission check. The more expensive the property, the more money the owner can save by keeping their property off market and using a wholesaler.

Something that helps you sell them. Run the numbers of their total savings and take-home cash. Compare it to what they would make with the real estate agent, but the realistic with them. Let them know that just because they list their property at a certain price with the real estate agent, that does not mean they are going to get that asking price.

Wholesalers usually buy houses as is. This is because a lot of times a lot of end buyers are real estate investors that are flipping houses. A lot of times this is perfect for the seller.

A common situation that we see is that the property owner can't afford to repair their house or their investment property. You, as a wholesaler, can offer them a price that is acceptable to them, gives you a profit, and also leaves room for your end buyer to spend money to repair and then re-sell for a profit.

If the house has a lot of problems or issues for the owner, especially if they live there and have no money for repairs, they might be motivated when hearing that. Just like if you are able to help an owner someone who is nearing foreclosure, by offering them a bail-out in the form of an assignable contract – or taking over "subject to".

In most real estate transactions that hit the market, buyers will try to get money back for repairs after the home inspection. This annoying step is completely avoided when you work with the wholesaler, because like I said I buy houses AS-IS.

Closing costs are another huge factor that eat into a seller's profits. Wholesalers most times pay all the closing costs. Remember, this is a cash deal so we don't have to pay some of the fees that would be on the HUD statement when a mortgage company or a bank is involved. In the previous post I discussed all the fees that you'll see at closing when you are going through a cash deal.

Tell them in a matter of fact way:

"When you work with me and my company, you get a whole team working to close on time and correctly. We're going close quickly, you're going to get all cash on closing, we're going to buy the property as-is so you're not spending any money - we're not renegotiating any deals and trying to get money taken off for repairs. This simple plain text contract is all there is. $50,000 cash to you in 45 days.

We're going to pay all your closing costs, assume all liabilities and issues with the house. The price that we offer you, is the price that is going to be deposited into your bank account to help solve all of your problems, there'll be no commissions taken out of that price.

Our maximum offer - is also a quick as-is and cash offer which might help to remove some of the stress out of your life."

Let them know that you are a professional so you can handle the issues that there are with the home, and it doesn't kill the deal for you – but for most other people these repairs will.

Tell them how the home inspector, and city inspector are going to red flag the issues you noted, but you can handle those issues. When you keep the deal off market with you there are no city inspectors or home inspectors needed.

Let them know that these repairs do cost money through and you need to account for that when you do the math and make the offer.

That's just how math works.

Make sure you walk the property with the seller if possible. Casually mention to yourself all of the negative aspects about the property. This is where it pays to be observant.

Take pictures of every space. Note which areas have bad or non-existent lighting and fans. Make sure you mention this loud enough for them to hear. Over time, the things you mention will add up in their head.

They are aware with the issues of the property, but they need to hear them all over again, so they start tallying the numbers up in their own head. They will start to tell themselves that, yes – these repairs and upgrades that are needed to sell the house at market price – they do cost money and they do add up.

AUTHORITY

If you follow all of the steps, I have been telling you about, and implementing them correctly, your clients will see you as a professional in your field. They will know you have authority just by the way you talk.

Don't be afraid to tell them "No." You are your own boss now, and this is your business.

When you walk through a seller's property with them, you should see yourself essentially as a professional property inspector. You are basically like a doctor, performing a full physical on the house. You're giving it a check-up to see if there are any issues.

If you find some, you document it and that's how it is. The facts are the facts, and you are an expert in finding out facts about property. You are also an expert at selling houses off the market, quickly. You are a master at assessing repairs and you always follow through on your word.

If you carry yourself with those facts in your head and strive to make them a reality – your clients will see you as a professional who is deserving of their trust in your authority.

They will trust that you are capable enough to follow through with the fancy words you've been telling them.

SEND THE PROPERTY TO YOUR BUYERS

You should have a large list of buyers and real estate investors by now. Put together a one page offering flyer with some pictures and pertinent information about the property and send it out to your buyers.

We have a winning template that we use that displays all the pertinent information that all serious investors want to know - in a visually appealing way.

Depending on the property, we'll put the cap rates or some other investor targeted information.

Your buyers may make offers, they may want to see more of the property and do some walkthroughs. Be prepared to show the property once you get the contract signed by the seller.

Assign the contract to a serious end buyer with the intent to close quickly on the property. They aren't serious until their deposit is in your bank account or the escrow account.

Once you have a serious buyer, and they make an offer that gives you a reasonable profit, sign the contracts.

Many clients will ask me if it's better to buy from a wholesaler, rather than go through an agent.

All I have to say is, just look at how the numbers work for you, don't worry about what the wholesaler potentially stands to make, do your due diligence and follow the cash flow.

Some buyers are investors who may try to cut you out of the deal. Unless you have the property under contract, do not send the address or the seller information to any of your buyers.

Don't tell anyone what you have the home under contract for either. They can make offers, but you aren't going to show your hand. You don't owe these people anything.

Don't take any buyer serious unless they have proof of funds or a pre-approval letter from a mortgage company.

If you break your own rules and make exceptions for all your clients, you won't be in business very long.

COLLECT YOUR DEPOSIT CHECK / ASSIGNMENT FEE

Your most interested party (end buyer) will be giving you offers and negotiating price with you. Once you both agree on a price that leaves you a reasonable profit it is time to sign on it and pay the deposit.

Agreement to Assign Contract for Sale and Purchase

Subject Property: ███████████████████████████

Legal Description: ███████████████

This agreement is made between Larkspur York Capital II, LLC (ASSIGNOR) and ███████████ (ASSIGNEE) regarding purchase of the above referenced SUBJECT PROPERTY.

Whereas Larkspur York Capital II, LLC (BUYER) has entered into a Purchase and Sales Agreement with ███ (SELLER) for the purchase of SUBJECT PROPERTY, and whereas BUYER wishes to assign its rights, interests and obligations in the Purchase and Sales Agreement, it is hereby agreed between ASSIGNOR and ASSIGNEE as follows:

1. ASSIGNEE shall pay ASSIGNOR a NON-REFUNDABLE assignment fee of $12,750 (payable $5,000 with signing of contract and $7,750 at close).

2. ASSIGNEE accepts all terms and conditions of the contract for Sale and Purchase between BUYER and SELLER in its entirety.

3. ASSIGNEE acknowledges receipt of legible copies of the original Contract for Sale and Purchase in its entirety including all Addendum(s) associated with this transaction.

4. Additional terms and conditions of this Assignment are as follows:

   a) This assignment contract is non-assignable without the express written consent of the ASSIGNOR. No changes to the Purchase Contract can be made without written Consent of BUYER.

   b) Disclosures and Acknowledgement:

   i) ASSIGNOR and affiliated associates make no warranty, expressed or implied, regarding inspection reports or other reports provided to ASSIGNEE by ASSIGNOR or third parties concerning this property.

   ii) ASSIGNEE acknowledges they are conducting a transaction dealing directly with ASSIGNOR for the purchase of SUBJECT PROPERTY. ASSIGNEE is not relying upon or being represented by a REAL ESTATE BROKERAGE in this transaction.

AGREED AND ACCEPTED

████████████ 04/23/2019   ███████ 4/23/2019
Assignee   Date   Assignor   Date

████████████   Joseph Coello
Print Name   Print Name

████████████ 04/23/2019
Assignee   Date

████████████
Print Name

The end buyer will sign your assignment of contract form which allows them to buy the rights of the contract from you. We have included the exact same form we use to assign contracts.

Once the contracts are signed, you should collect a non-refundable (or refundable depending on the deal) deposit check from the end buyer. Get all copies of all signed contracts over to your lawyer as soon as you get them signed. You want to make sure your lawyer and title company have the correct forms on time!

A quick example wholesale deal would go like this. You get a property under an assignable contract from a seller for $50,000. You find an end-buyer for $65,000. You collect $5,000 as a non-refundable deposit from the end buyer once you assign the contract to him.

You will receive the other $10,000 after closing, with the grand total listed as an assignment fee on the HUD-1 statement during closing.

Don't spend your deposit check when you get the money, hold this fee in escrow until the property closes, even if it is non-refundable.

I don't like to be in the habit of taking people's deposit checks, unless they are tying up a deal from closing for weeks or months and then back out - it is really all circumstantial. I would just be cautious to burn any bridges when you can easily return the deposit and move on to the next deal.

AFTER YOU ASSIGN THE CONTRACT

Congratulations, you are getting really close to completing your first deal. If you followed all the steps up to this point correctly, you are almost finished, but you still have a few more minor details to handle before you can focus on the next deal.

Scan the original copy and get it saved in a safe place for your records. You'll need to get a copy of the full contract package to both the buyer's and seller's attorney.

Give them both a call to introduce yourself and tell them that you look forward to working with them to ensure a smooth closing. Send the forms to attorney and/or title company to the email that they gave you. If you need to hand deliver these forms, then do so to get the job done, also take the opportunity to meet the attorney

If you got all of the contracts signed properly, and you got all the correct forms over to the attorney then your job may be finished. In the best situations, you just need to wait until closing and collect your final payment.

Continue to keep open lines of communication with everyone involved until the closing date.

In more time-consuming situations, you may need to assist the seller in getting the required documents to the attorney.

Be prepared to go the extra mile in this step to set yourself above the competition.

MANAGING THE DEAL

If you made mistakes on your contract or did not get some forms signed, the attorney will let you know. It is important to have a good relationship with the attorneys you work with.

If there is an issue with something, make sure you take it upon yourself to handle it and expedite the process. If your seller's need to re-sign a form, or if something needs to get sent to the buyers, or buyer's attorney – make sure it gets done by doing it yourself.

Make sure the property closes. Follow up with the attorneys, the seller and the end buyers. Maintain good communications and make sure everyone is doing what they need to keep the deal process moving.

If people don't return your phone call, follow up!

The standard closing process starts with the signing of a purchase agreement. The title search and the survey's get ordered and the title companies start working on determining if the property has a clean title to be transferred.

If there is a mortgage being taken out, the bank will send an appraiser to the house to determine the value and the bank will also begin their final underwriting process.

From there the Attorney or title company may need to remedy the title or do some things called "title curatives"

These all allow for title insurance to be issued. If title insurance can't be issued sometimes the seller will need to buy an "owners policy" to essentially guarantee that the title is clear.

Once the title is clear and title insurance gets ordered. Usually now the deed starts to get prepared. Once this document is typed up and ready and the money is fully allocated to buy the house – a closing date is set.

Once the property closes, you will get the last portion of your assignment fee in the form of a certified check.

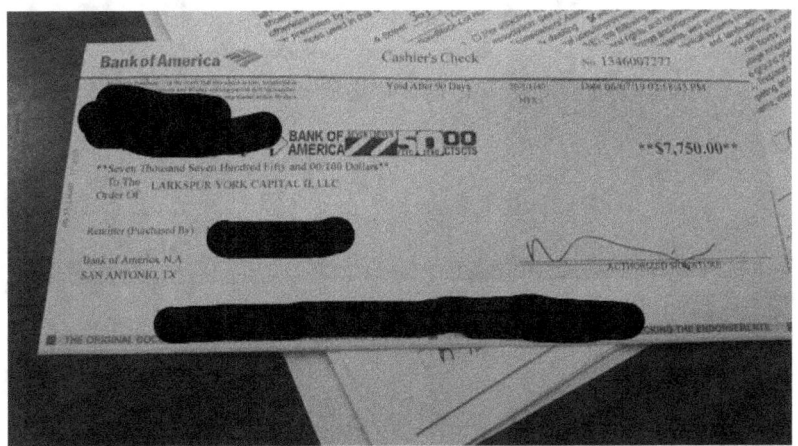

FINDING THE NEXT ONE

Once the property closes - congratulations you closed your first deal. Focus on building your deal pipeline so you can develop a constant income stream.

Start looking for your next deal as soon as you get the deposit check on your first deal. You should have a constantly growing rolodex, and several appointments every week to look at houses.

You're only failing yourself if you start something and quit. There is no one else here to hold you accountable but yourself. Make sure you put your full effort into this, and you will be rewarded.

These are the broad steps that you need to take if you want to get involved with wholesaling or wholetailing. In all fields there is a small percent of people who are succeeding. If you want to do just a few deals a year, the opportunity for you to do that is endless.

If you want to make a serious income stream from wholesaling, you need to do set up your business framework to handle multiple deals and have an abundant, sustainable mindset.

BEING YOUR OWN BOSS

Real Estate can give you freedom that you've never had before. It can be tough to stay on track when you don't have anyone but yourself to answer to.

Don't forget that you are a business owner now, and when you make money, no one is taking taxes out for you. You need to stay on top of tracking your income and business expenses. Consult with an accountant to best assess your personal tax situation.

It takes discipline and self-motivation to excel as a wholesaler. Set goals and targets for yourself to reach. Make your goals tangible and pave the way to your endgame.

FINDING A MENTOR

The road to successful wholesaling is a very foggy and unmonitored path. You won't get much help from other wholesalers in your area because you are direct competition to them in most cases. The people who are successful in wholesaling, and other aspects of real estate are often very busy.

Don't expect to get a free mentorship from a busy professional without providing them value in some way as well. Offer to do clerical work for them and learn the ropes while you work if you have to.

The best way to succeed is to directly follow the footsteps of someone who has successfully done these exact same deals.

There are a few ways to find yourself a good real estate investing mentor.

1. Join a Real Estate Investor Association for as low as $300 a month.
2. Hire someone to be your mentor.
3. If the above two options are too expensive and you're still struggling to find a mentor, email me personally at coellojoseph@gmail.com and I promise I will do my professional best to introduce you to one.

www.ingramcontent.com/pod-product-compliance
Lightning Source LLC
Chambersburg PA
CBHW071416210526
45465CB00001B/421